IMAGES
of America

REDLANDS

IMAGES
of America
REDLANDS

Larry E. Burgess
Nathan D. Gonzales

ARCADIA
PUBLISHING

Published by Arcadia Publishing
Charleston, South Carolina

Library of Congress Catalog Card Number: 2004101544

For all general information contact Arcadia Publishing at:
Telephone 843-853-2070
Fax 843-853-0044
E-mail sales@arcadiapublishing.com
For customer service and orders:
Toll-Free 1-888-313-2665

Visit us on the Internet at www.arcadiapublishing.com

CONTENTS

PREFACE

Collaboration made some of the greatest teams in history: Thomas Jefferson and John Adams on the Declaration of Independence; Gilbert and Sullivan in operettas; Lewis and Clark as explorers; Rogers and Hammerstein in music. While great results were attained, so were severe fractures. Jefferson and Adams did not speak for decades; Lewis committed suicide and Clark went his own course; Gilbert and Sullivan broke up amid acrimony and volatility. Only Rogers and Hammerstein maintained their idyllic relationship—until the families started penning memoirs after their deaths.

Fortunately, we seem to have eluded the fate of past collaborators and now present our effort in behalf of Redlands still friends, colleagues, and without ever uttering a disparaging word. So euphoric are we, that there has even been talk of another effort.

Larry brought longevity and decades of involvement with the history of Redlands to the project, first as founding archivist and then head of special collections at A.K. Smiley Public Library, a position he has held since 1972. Nathan, a younger and more recent addition to the staff (1999), supplied perspective through fresh eyes and a unique talent for blending technical computer expertise with layout capability.

More important to the story is that both Larry and Nathan, as trained historians with graduate degrees, seek to bring to this pictorial overview of Redlands (or as Frank E. Moore, the late editor of the Redlands Daily Facts called it, "Our Town"), a blend of tradition and new perspectives.

From the thousands of photographs, ephemera, and objects in the Heritage Room of the Smiley Library, we have culled a sampling of images and accompanying text that we hope will give a sense of place and of the evolution of the historical process. The progress of history and our part in it is dramatically shown by photographs of sites, people, and events that we remember. "Gosh, wasn't that just the other day?" we ask incredulously of a building now gone or a street corner altered.

We hope the reader will enjoy this book and find it a useful tool in helping to understand where we have been, so that we might better understand where we are going.

—Larry E. Burgess and Nathan D. Gonzales
March 2004

INTRODUCTION

Redlands, California, named in 1881 for its reddish adobe soil, was founded as the result of collaboration by two young Connecticut Yankees, 26-year-old Frank E. Brown and 30-year-old Edward Judson. Both had read the seductive and popular 1873 book, *California for Health, Pleasure and Residence* by Charles Nordhoff, and were particularly intrigued by Chapter Twelve, which devoted itself entirely to the San Bernardino Valley. Brown, a senior at Yale, and his friend Judson, working on Wall Street in Manhattan, turned the pages thinking of Horace Greeley's admonition to "Go West Young Man" and seeing out their window the swirling winter snow.

Arriving in Lugonia, now north Redlands, the two carefully laid their plans to establish a colony of emigrants from the snowbound East and Midwest who could plant profitable groves of Washington navel oranges, prosper in the salubrious climate, and enjoy the sweeping views of the San Bernardino Mountains.

The young colony's evolution came quickly. As Edward Judson noted, "The place began to grow and the first we knew we had a town on our hands." Early settlers from the years 1885 to 1886 included the Chicago Colony, who named its streets—Dearborn, La Salle, Wabash, Lincoln, and State—for their hometown. They were succeeded by people from the East Coast and New England. In 1888 the town incorporated, swallowing Lugonia. By 1889, the arrival of the famous twin Smiley brothers, educators and New York resort owners, proved that people could make the difference, as Frank Brown expressed, in that "the coming of these eastern people, these Smileys, will make Redlands known as the coming spot."

As a tourist destination, the Smiley brothers' Cañon Crest Park, also known as Smiley Heights, drew thousands of tourists a year from 1890 through 1930. The Smileys opened the gates of their estate, with its 200 acres of horticultural delights and magnificent views, freely to tourists who came via tallyhos to tour this Eden and then often ate at the local restaurants, stayed at the hotels, and sent back home to the folks in Des Moines and Boston postcards about this remarkable town.

Redlands was able to build upon Judson and Brown's vision, and especially Brown's civil engineering ability, in the form of the Big Bear Dam (a designated engineering wonder of the modern world by the American Society of Civil Engineers), which guaranteed a water supply at Big Bear reservoir for Redlands.

Thanks to his personal interest in horticulture, Redlands co-founder Edward Judson saw to it that hundreds of trees were given to early settlers. His personal favorite, the palm, along

7

with other tree varieties, were planted, thus beginning Redlands's long-standing love affair with trees.

By the turn of the 20th century, Redlands grew from a few hundred to nearly 5,000 residents. President McKinley visited Redlands in 1901, making it his "California Welcome." When President Theodore Roosevelt made his first visit to California in 1903, Redlands was his first stop. By 1910 the town was shipping out the greatest number of Washington navels in the citrus belt.

Not all history is rosy or easy. Disastrous freezes struck in 1913 and again in the 1920s, 1930s and in 1978. There was a Christmas Day earthquake in 1899 and a flood in Mill Creek and the Santa Ana River in 1938. Sleepy Redlands had a murder-suicide love triangle in 1890 involving the owners of the Windsor Hotel, an anti-Chinese mob attempting a riot in 1893, and even a red-light area developing on Sylveria Street (now Third) near the railroad tracks. Citizens viewed with amazement the obliteration of half of downtown for a mall in the 1970s.

But the town's extensive photographic history records more positive images, such as the owners of the more than 30 citrus packing houses, as well as the workers. Millionaires in their wonder mansions are captured on glass slides and on negatives, as are school children, members of organizations, tourists, the city's official fly catcher, a Chinese family at the McKinley parade in 1901—all part of the historic fabric.

However, history is as much a story of what has been lost as it is one of what has been gained. Redlands is rightly proud of its history and heritage, but those coming after the mid-1970s may be shocked to discover that perhaps half of the truly "great" homes of Redlands have been lost to fire, demolition, or neglect. Some two-thirds of the commercial structures of the community have been demolished to make way for new developments or have been so badly "modernized" that they are no longer recognizable as historic buildings.

In Redlands, a strong tradition of philanthropy is captured. When Albert K. Smiley presented the library building and park to the city, he did so with borrowed money. Other citizens came to the fore. A building was provided for the Redlands Bowl. A museum to Abraham Lincoln and the Civil War would become part of the city's educational assets and the only such edifice to a president built by a private individual. It is also the only museum and library dedicated to this cause west of the Mississippi River. Parks were created and given to the public. Private homes became museums housing cultural and musical collections.

In 1906, when the Northern Baptists sought a site for a new college in Southern California, Redlands citizens offered money, land, city support, and enthusiasm. By November 1907, the infant University of Redlands had its own site and a board of trustees.

Important Redlands notes include the Redlands Day Nursery, California's oldest; the first generation of three-phase electrical power in the world; the creation of the first white line to divide opposing lanes of traffic on a city street; the oldest musical organization in the state, the Spinet; one of the oldest continuously meeting literary societies in America, the Fortnightly Club; and the oldest continuously run outdoor free professional music concert series in America, the Redlands Summer Music Festival at the Redlands Bowl. The dominant spirit of Grace Stewart Mullen refused to give in to naysayers when she proposed in 1924 a free concert featuring professionals. More than 100,000 people enjoy her legacy each summer season.

What these pages show are views about community, and the people, places, and events that have influenced the type of town that Redlands has become. But like all things, not everything can be shown or described, and the reader who wants to learn more may wish to investigate the collections and archives of material housed in the Heritage Room of A.K. Smiley Public Library.

Without doubt it was Clarence G. White, in his remarks donating the Redlands Bowl Prosellis building to the city in 1930, who best captured the essence that has defined Redlands:

We hope that each man, woman and child who has been impelled to do more for this community than he has been compelled to do will feel that he has contributed to the building of this Prosellis.

No city lives by taxes alone. The nearer it comes to that condition, the more drab and monotonous its existence is.

Many of us take for granted the immense amount of free personal service that goes into making a town like Redlands.

If this building emphasizes such service to you, and the need for all to help keep Redlands at its best, Mrs. White and I will remember this occasion with full hearts.

What this building is good for is just what you and I make it good for.

By itself it is only an ornament. If we citizens give it a meaning, it is a challenge and maybe a responsibility.

We hope that such good citizens, if they have not received a full recognition of work well done, will feel that here is recognition, co-operation, and perhaps some reward.

The dedication tablet on the building reads, "A thank offering for all who have made Redlands a good place to live in."

From orange groves and mountain views, to community organizations and thriving business, Redlands truly has made itself the "Jewel of the Inland Empire."

Even though the "snowbirds" of the East and Midwest came to Redlands to avoid snow, they weren't always successful. Downtown Redlands is blanketed with snow in the "Snow of '49," in this view looking south on Orange Street from the Redlands Glass House.

A History and Description OF THE

BARTON RANCH

home of the ORANGE

LEMONS

.Olives, Limes,
Figs, Almonds,
Raisins, Apricots, Peaches, Pears etc.

LOCATED IN

San Bernardino County,
CALIFORNIA.

LOS ANGELES LITHOGRAPHIC CO.

Ben Barton purchased the south eastern section of Rancho San Bernardino in 1857. Barton was among the land owners from whom Judson and Brown bought tracts of land to develop for the Redlands Colony in 1881. By 1890, the Barton Land and Water Company advertised the remainder of the Barton Ranch for sale in 10-acre lots.

One

BEFORE REDLANDS

The Zanja, dug by Cahuilla Indians under Chief Solano with Pedro Alvarez serving as "engineer" from San Gabriel Mission, winds its way to the Barton Ranch (now Nevada Street at Barton Road) around 1885. Coursing its way for 11 miles from Mill Creek, it served an *estancia* (commonly known as the Asistencia) of the mission.

Looking down on the east San Bernardino Valley, one almost feels the primordial earth. Long before the smog of the 20th century, a clean, low-strata marine layer often would shroud the valley, most notably in June.

Members of the San Manuel band of the Serrano Mission Indians are shown at their "Big House" near Highland around 1890. The structure served as the center for tribal discussion and rule making.

The Barton house appears on the left with the adobe ruins of the 1830 *estancia* of San Gabriel Mission on the right. In earlier times this site was Guachama, a Cahuilla Indian village.

South Carolinian Dr. Ben Barton arrived in the San Bernardino Valley in the 1850s and built this house in 1867 on a knoll at his ranch. The house, with its mansard roof, observation tower, and a separate cook house, served as a social and political center.

J.D.B. Stillman joined the 1849 California Gold Rush and came to the east San Bernardino Valley in 1879, settling in Lugonia (now north Redlands) where he laid out a 100-acre vineyard. This 1885 view from his house looks north to Mt. Harrison. Today the site is the University of Redlands.

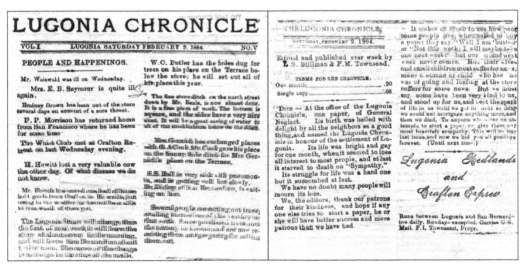

This shows both sides of the short-lived *Lugonia Chronicle*. The small-format newspaper was intended to be four pages, but was cut back to two in January 1884. The paper above may well be the last issue, the article reading "DIED—At the office of the Lugonia Chronicle, one paper, of General Neglect . . . Its life was bright and gay for one month, when it seemed to lose all interest to most people, and at last starved to death on 'Sympathy.'"

Two

THE FIRST WE KNEW WE HAD A TOWN ON OUR HANDS

George Cook opened this store, its third location, in Lugonia in 1882 on the south side of Colton Avenue at Orange Street. It housed the Lugonia post office and telephone station. The photo is from about 1890, when Benton O. Johnson & Company occupied the business.

Prospect House, on a hill off Cajon Street at Highland Avenue (now Prospect Park), was the "Redlands" colony's first hotel, in 1882. It was run by Dr. Ellen B. Seymour, cousin of Frank E. Brown, co-founder of Redlands. For three years its water was hauled in barrels from the Zanja.

This view of what would become downtown Redlands shows a livery stable on east State Street near Sixth Street, c. 1888.

This is State Street in 1887 looking east to the intersection of Orange Street. The Union Bank building is on the northeast corner.

Ralph Richey, left, and John P. Fisk, Redlands's first real estate and insurance broker, appear in Fisk's office on the second floor of the Union Bank. Fisk arrived from Beloit, Wisconsin, and his first real estate transaction was selling the Barton Ranch. His most famous transaction was selling the Smiley brothers the land that would become Smiley Heights.

Lugonia, founded in 1870, was originally called "Sunnyside." When an area in Riverside also claimed that name, the new designation became "Lugonia," in honor of the Lugo family, who owned the San Bernardino Rancho in the 1840s.

Downtown began to take form by the late 1880s. This is State Street looking west from between Fifth and Sixth Streets.

Later the site of the 1970s Redlands Mall, this *c.* 1890 location on west State Street features the Windsor Hotel and next to it the Odd Fellows building.

Scipio Craig's weekly Citrograph newspaper, printed on book paper, was famous throughout Southern California and was exhibited at the 1893 Chicago World's Fair. This second location on Fifth Street shows Craig, second from right, with his crew.

Founded in 1890 as a weekly, the *Redlands Facts* turned daily in 1892. The composing room where type was handset is shown here in about 1895 at its 15 East State Street location.

The Citrograph.

EXTRA.

VOL. 3.   REDLANDS, CAL., NOV. 27, 1888.   No.——

HURRAH !

For the City of Redlands ! !

Incorporation Carried by a Rousing Majority.

A Triumphal March of Progressive Principles.

Mossbacks and Silurians Will Now Take a Back Seat.

153 Majority for Progress and Prosperity.

There is Nothing Too Good for Redlands, the Phenomenal City of Wonderful California.

Yesterday was a red-letter day in the Annals of Redlands. For days the all absorbing topic had been "incorporation." Nothing else c uld be heard. Business men forgot their customers in the absorbing theme. Professional men neglected their clients to argue the case. Farmers and fruit growers stopped their

with as much persistence as those of the sterner sex. Everything was in a fever of excitement which only grew more intense as the fateful day grew nearer and closer. Both the advocates of incorporation and those opposed were busily engaged in button-holing every voter and then "marking him down" on their private lists. Every recreant citizen was assailed on all sides, until not a citizen, entitled to vote, but was gotten on the Great Register.

On Friday of last week, the opponents of incorporation went to San Bernardino and got out a circular appealing to the votors not to saddle upon themselves the enormous burden of taxation incumbent on an incorporated city. Appeals were made in every manner possible. To offset this the CITROGRAPH issued a special incorporation edition on Saturday, setting forth in a calm, reasoning way, the great benefits that would accrue from incorporation. And thus the matter was left to the intelligent voter.

Yesterday the day was ushered in with a fine, drizzling rain that promised anything but comfort for pedestrians. But nothing could damp the ardor of the voter. Promptly at six o'clock the polls were opened with E. A. Ball as Judge, and Lathrop and Peller as judges. H. W. Camp and F. F. Harp acted as clerks.

Voters commenced depositing their ballots early and by 9 o'clock there were 64 ballots cast and over 160 by noon. Every voter was looked after, carriages being sent hither and thither bringing in those who were unable to walk, or who did not care to brave the mud. The result was that 284 ballots were cast, six more than were cast at the presidential election twenty days ago, although the cutting down of the election precinct into city lines left out more than thirty voters. The increase comes in from those voters who were only a few days too late for the presidential election.

The result of the magnificent work done by those most interested may be seen by the following

SUMMARY:

Total number of votes cast	284
For Incorporation	216
Against Incorporation	68
Majority	153

TRUSTEES.

E. G. Judson	257
J. B. Glover	251
B. W. Cave	244
C. N. Andrews	243
H. H. Sinclair	203
R. C. Shepherd	132

The first five being elected.

FOR CLERK.

L. W. Clark	189
F. J. Higinbotham	89

FOR MARSHAL.

Wm. C. Brumagim	147
W. S. Warren	108
W. D. Williams	24
Brumagim's Plurality	39

FOR TREASURER.

F. P. Morrison	273

No opposition

There were a few scattering votes in several places, but it is not necessary to give the figures here.

The result of this election proves several things.

First:—It proves that our people are educated and intelligent, and that they are perfectly capable of reasoning and judging for themselves on any point of public policy that may come up.

Second:—That our people are not to be shunted off of the main line of progress on to the side track of silurianism by any specious arguments gotten up on the outside by men who have no vote on the question at issue.

Third:—That the people of Redlands have not one particle of animosity for the people of Lugonia. This is evidenced by the fact that two Lugonians were elected out of five Trustees. Lugonia was—considering the vote—only entitled to one representative. Redlands votes gave her two showing that there was every desire on the part of Redlanders to accord Lugonia even more than was her just due. Let this incident forever set at rest the foul slanders that have been circulated by a ouple of Lugoniaites that Redlands was "trying to hog it all"

As it now stands we have seen, after a stormy and tempestuous courtship, Miss Fair Lugonia wedded to Mr. Stalwart Redlands. As Miss Fair—by the act of marriage—has merged her name and individuality into that of Mr. Stalwart, so will Mr. Stalwart love and cherish the pride of his manly bosom, and suffer no breath of calumny to rest upon good name. That will be defended with his strong right arm to the last gasp.

And as the progeny of this well matched couple, we shall have Peace, Prosperity, Progress and Fame. Let us see to it that the good name of this wedding be spread abroad all over the world, so that those who are weary of the rude buffetings of the snow storm, the cyclone, the thunder bolt, may all find here that rest and peace and comfort and prosperity that will form a fitting prelude to translation to that home of eternal peace prepared for all who have lived lives that would fit them for eternal enjoyment.

TO-NIGHT—GRAND RATIFICATION.

There will be a grand ratification meeting tonight. Rally at State and Orange streets tonight and bring your shot guns, horns, whistles and anything else that will make a noise

Redlands incorporated by a vote of the residents of Redlands and Lugonia on November 26, 1888, unifying the two communities.

21

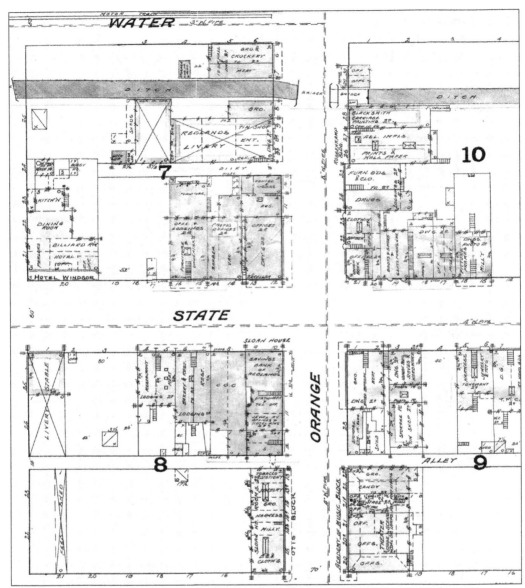

Downtown Redlands was really taking shape by the time this Dakin Publishing Company Insurance Map was created in January 1893. The first insurance maps depicting Redlands were drawn by the Sanborn-Perris Map Company (later Sanborn Map Company) and date to April 1888, seven months before the vote for incorporation. These insurance maps, which cover built-up areas of the city from 1888 to 1961, are invaluable tools for researchers looking at individual property histories, town growth and development, cultural and use change, size and type of construction, and myriad other uses.

Turn-of-the-century masons rest among the stones they have cut. From foundations to chimneys, curbs to caps, and walkways to irrigation ditches and retaining walls, more than a dozen men used stones from Mill Creek and Santa Ana Canyons for their artistry.

The farriers of the Sherrard and Dorr blacksmith shop pose for a photograph in 1886 between making horseshoes and fitting them on the horse.

The Seymour Brothers planing mill at the corner of Stuart and Fifth Streets supplied the lumber for many of Redlands's homes and commercial buildings, including the Morey House, "Hermosa Vista."

D.M. Donald, prominent Redlands builder, is shown with his crew in 1902. Donald built such structures as Kimberly Crest, the Burrage Mansion "Monte Vista," and A.K. Smiley Public Library.

Three

THE COMING SPOT

The southwest corner of State and Orange Streets as it looked in 1896. For 10 years, mules of the Redlands Street Railway pulled streetcars from Fifth and State Streets to points in south Redlands. The building on the corner is the First National Bank of Redlands, designed by T.R. Griffith, architect of Smiley Library.

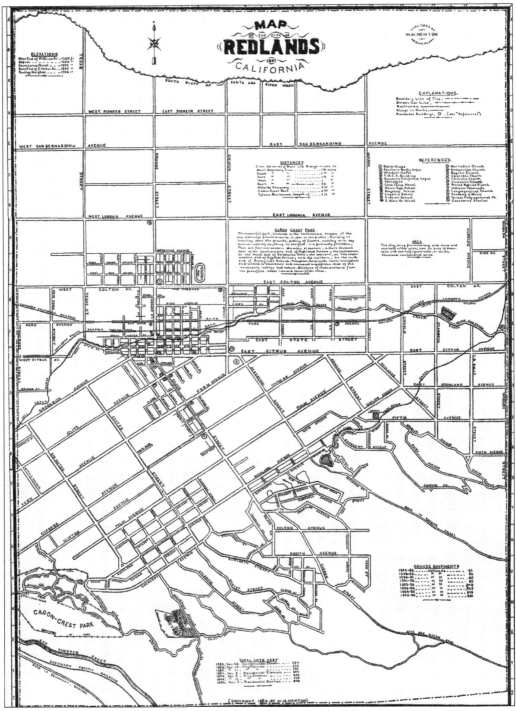

W.M. Newton published this "Map of the City of Redlands" in 1897. The layout of the city was well established by this point, with the only real changes being the addition of new streets in the large open areas as orange groves were developed into housing subdivisions.

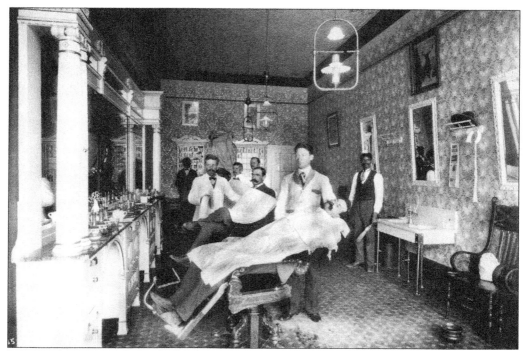

J.C. Bingham opened this barbershop in 1892 at 221 Orange Street south of Water Street (now Redlands Boulevard). Note the cuspidor in the lower right, a standard item in shops of the day.

Here is Orange Street as it appeared around 1900. This shot looks south from the Southern Pacific Railroad crossing, between the Santa Fe tracks and Redlands Boulevard. The YMCA/City Hall building is at the far end of Orange Street. In the street stand the sons of Redlands photographer E.N. James.

Three horse teams and wagons are loaded with cargo in front of the Palace Livery Stable on Orange Street, across the street and south from the Santa Fe Railway Station, *c*. 1900.

From City Hall, formerly the YMCA building, this view of Orange Street around 1900 looks north. The Fisher Building is on the right; the triangle formed by the intersection of Orange, Cajon, and Citrus Streets is on the left. George Hinckley painted a white line to divide lanes here at Cajon and Vine Streets, according to Popular Mechanics magazine in August 1911.

This is a view of State Street in 1903 looking east from Fourth Street. The Chandler Building is nearing completion in the distance.

From the start, flowers were part of the pioneer Redlands scene. Hedge rows of roses became popular along the streets bordering orange groves. Hockridge Nurseries during the early part of the 20th century supplied the needs of many a Redlands green thumb.

Postmaster William N. Tisdale moved the Redlands Post Office from Orange and Water Streets (now Redlands Boulevard) to this building on January 31, 1903. Here the post office remained until 1918. The building's upper floors consisted of a large meeting hall and offices for different lodges and clubs in town. The building was later named for Guy Chandler, who owned the structure and operated the Chandler Furniture Company. In 1971 the building was condemned and razed the following year. The vacant site became a "pocket park" in 1978, later named for longtime planning commissioner Ed Hales.

El Amigo del Hogar ("The Friend of the Home") was a Redlands Spanish-language paper published twice a month by Ascensión G. Lerma at 238 Webster Street. Volume one, issue four, pictured left, is the only copy that has survived of this small paper.

Jose Rivera served as Redlands's constable from 1888 to 1934. Born in Pomona in 1861, he lived in the San Bernardino Valley before Judson and Brown arrived to found Redlands in 1881. He was known and respected by Redlanders as "a man of understanding, good heart, and to be trusted."

The First National Bank of Redlands was originally formed as the Bank of the East San Bernardino Valley, and was incorporated in March 1887 in Lugonia. Seeing that development was settling in what would become downtown Redlands, the bank moved from Lugonia to Redlands in June 1888, and changed its name to reflect its new location. In 1892 a new building was constructed on the southwest corner of State and Orange Streets, and in 1914 the bank opened this Classical Revival structure.

The National Bank system provided for the use of paper money by allowing National Banks to purchase U.S. securities. In exchange, currency bearing their name was issued to those banks and would then enter circulation. In 1914 the Federal Reserve Note was introduced, and eventually replaced the National Bank notes.

The Union Bank also began in March 1887 at the northeast corner of State and Orange Streets, and in 1904 became the Redlands National Bank. In 1922 it was purchased by the Hellman Bank of Los Angeles, eventually becoming part of Bank of America. In 1929 the building was razed and a new Art Deco structure was built, which was demolished in turn in 1959 in favor of a Rexall Drug Store to be built on its site. Below are the lobby and cashiers' windows around 1905.

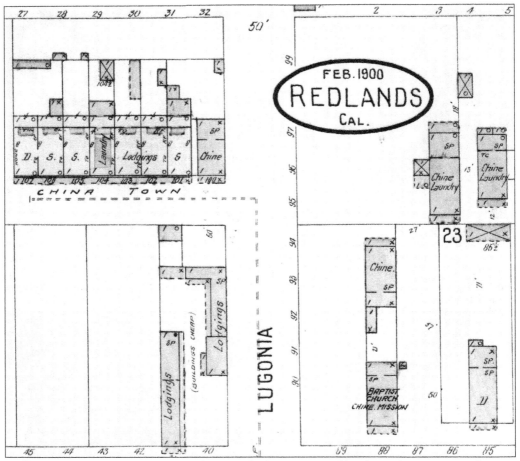

Redlands Chinatown began to take shape in the late 1880s and by the mid-1890s was a thriving community. Chinese provided inexpensive labor in the western United States, and surrounding communities, including San Bernardino and Riverside, had Chinatowns. This Sanborn Map Company map from 1900 shows Chinatown at its zenith. The east-west street on which the buildings front was later named Oriental Avenue and extended in each direction. The street here named Lugonia was realigned and called Eureka Street. Redlands Chinatown was active until the end of 1922, when the last resident moved out. Chinese residents continued to live in Redlands, but the days of strictly ethnic enclaves were over.

Elias Everett photographed the interior of the First National Bank of Redlands in February 1900. Interesting to today's observer is the sign to the right of the cashier's window, a bank advertisement to its Chinese customers stating that they could send money to Shanghai and Hong Kong at a good rate of exchange, and also that bank accounts with immediate availability of funds for withdrawal were available.

Benjamin S. Stephenson, the first jeweler in Redlands, moved his shop from 16 East State Street, where it had stood since the 1880s, to this building on Fifth Street between Citrus Avenue and State Street in 1905. It also served as his family's residence.

Joseph J. Thamann ran his billiard hall and cigar shop at 220 (now 120) Orange Street. Billiards was a popular game when this picture was taken in 1910, a time when there were seven different halls in Redlands.

The Oyama Pool Room on Central Avenue (now Redlands Boulevard) at Fourth Street was one of a number of Japanese-run businesses present in Redlands in the early 1900s.

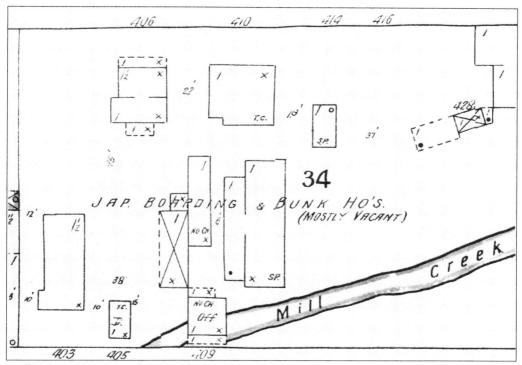

Redlands's Japanese residents worked predominantly in agriculture, although several ran businesses that catered to the Japanese population. This Sanborn Map from 1915 shows that the area on Redlands Boulevard near Eleventh Street was clearly cheap housing for the labor force. At this time there was also a Japanese employment office on State Street at Ninth, as well as other forms of recreation, like pool rooms, for the mostly male population.

In 1915 the Japanese members of the Redlands community joined together to present to the City of Redlands 200 cherry trees in honor of the coronation of His Imperial Majesty, the Emperor of Japan. The Taisho Emperor ascended to the throne in 1912. A large banquet was held at the Casa Loma Hotel, with numerous Redlands dignitaries as well as leaders of the Japanese community in attendance when the proclamation and gift were made, November 10, 1915. Sadly, the trees died due to a blight some years later.

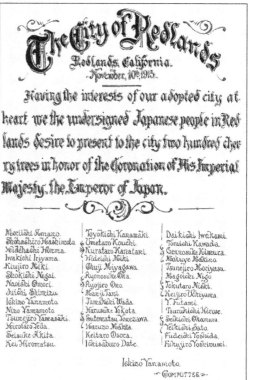

Arriving in Redlands in 1888, Albert Osbun became involved in several businesses. Pictured here is the Osbun and Parker machine shop on Central Avenue.

In 1906 A. Osbun opened an automobile agency at the Ironworks. First he sold Cadillacs, then the Tourist, the Mitchell, the Apperson, and finally the Ford. Following Osbun's death in 1935, the Ford Agency was taken on by son Ben Osbun Sr.

Shown here is the milk processing room of the Model Creamery, another of A. Osbun's family-run enterprises. It was located at 114–116 East State Street.

This is Orange Street in the mid-1920s seen from the second floor of the Union Bank. This view looks north to the intersection of Central and Orange Streets. At the far end of the street is an inbound Pacific Electric "Red Car."

Harry Beal owned a successful stage and car line catering to San Bernardino Mountain tourists. Beal, pictured here in 1914, was the son of Martha Embers and Israel Beal, who came to the valley in the 1850s and 1860s, respectively. Beal was also a musician, and his nephew Charles became a well-regarded jazz pianist, playing for actress Mary Martin, among others.

The Colored Citizen was a monthly gazette published in Redlands by Robert H. Harbert beginning with this issue, July 1, 1905. The last known extant copy dates to December 1906. Included on the Fourth of July–themed cover are Abraham Lincoln, George Washington, Booker T. Washington, Theodore Roosevelt, and Frederick Douglass. Little did Harbert know that nearly 10 years later Booker T. Washington would visit Redlands, speaking at the Contemporary Club.

Israel Beal's son Charles married Mabel Harbert. They and their family and friends were part of the Harbert Orchestra, which played for parties and church events in Redlands and Riverside. Shown here, from left to right, are as follows: (sitting center) Mabel Harbert; (front row) R.H. Harbert (director), Rosa D. Harbert, and Lola Harbert; (back row) Robert H. Harbert Jr., James Nicholson, Eddie Carter, Charles Arthur Beal, Harry Beal, and W.J. Thomas.

John Van Mouwerik is emblematic of the large Dutch colony that settled in Redlands between 1915 and 1930. Born in Holland, he settled in Redlands and by 1928 took over the Brookside Dairy business. Dutch churches and, for a time, instruction in the Dutch language marked this important immigrant community.

Formerly the Safeway store on the southwest corner of Citrus Avenue and Fifth Street, this site became an independent market in 1951. The building was razed for a business block, later the third City Hall.

Christmas decorations adorn State Street in 1955. The view from La Posada shows F.W. Woolworth at the southeast corner of State and Orange Streets. At one time Woolworth's was the largest variety chain in the world.

Shown here is another view of East State Street in 1967, just a few years before many of the buildings in downtown were razed or their facades radically changed in the quest for "modernization."

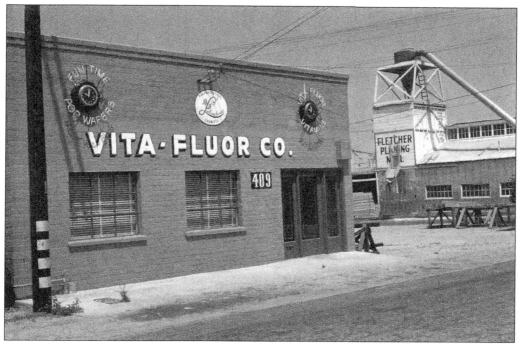

Here is a seldom seen view of the industrial side of Redlands. In this late 1960s photograph, a vitamin plant and a planing mill are shown on Fifth Street north of the Santa Fe Railway tracks.

Hudlow's was a well-known and popular establishment on Redlands Boulevard at Seventh Street. This image is from a book of matches, with the matches in the shape of bottles that were labeled Jim Beam, California Wine, Gin, Beer, Scotch, Champagne, and Brandy. The site became a bank parking lot.

Dining establishments that served liquor were rare in Redlands. During the 1950s and 1960s, people looking for a meal and a drink often landed at Pinky's, on the south side of Redlands Boulevard, just west of Orange Street. State Highway 99 came through Redlands in the late 1930s, spurring a string of successful restaurants, including Phil's Charcoal Broiler, farther west on the boulevard, which hosted the likes of Frank Sinatra and other Hollywood celebrities on their way to Palm Springs.

W. Lawrence Gill founded the Gill Storage Battery Company in 1920. He invented and perfected a storage battery for automobiles and aircraft far ahead of anything available at the time. His Redlands plant was located on Citrus Avenue and Sixth Street beginning in 1929. Tragically, this plant burned to the ground in 1950. Teledyne later acquired the company and continues to produce Gill Batteries.

This is a view of Downtown Redlands in the 1960s. Running north (bottom, left corner) is Cajon Street, turning to become Orange Street, and then Interstate 10 at the top right.

A dog poses by the water "dog bar" at Milton Gair's men's clothing store on Orange Street in the Academy of Music building, adjacent to the alley between State Street and Citrus Avenue. In the mid 1950s Gair's moved to East State Street and created a new "dog bar."

Hatfield Buick, founded by Bert S. Hatfield in 1911, had by 1962 moved to a site on East Redlands Boulevard. Shown here, from left to right, are Bert and sons John and Bob with Mayor Waldo Burroughs looking on. Hatfield Buick is the oldest Buick dealership in the United States.

46

Up until the 1970s and 1980s, drug stores often had lunch counters. The counter at Winn's Drugs, on the northwest corner of Colton Avenue at Orange Street, was known for its famous milk shakes and chocolate cokes, a place where people gathered to chat, gossip, and drink coffee. Carole Ley ran "Carole's Corner," below, at Winn's, and was noted for her fresh baked pies.

Succeeding Angelo's Red Carpet restaurant, the Tartan was located at the southeast corner of Fifth Street and Redlands Boulevard. A new building was constructed across Fifth Street in 1974 and the restaurant fixtures and furniture were all transplanted. The former site is now a parking lot.

The groundbreaking ceremony for the Redlands Mall was held on December 10, 1975. Six square blocks of historic downtown were leveled and a new enclosed mall arose on the site.

Four

AGRICULTURE AND THE ORANGE: CITRUS IS KING

Frank W. Moore's Elephant Orchards was representative of the local citrus industry, which began with the introduction of the Washington navel orange (the eating orange) in the 1870s and prospered until the 1950s. More than two dozen packing houses and 15,000 acres of fruit orchards employed many people.

Before Redlands became the "world's largest" producer of navel oranges, table grapes and wine grapes were king. In 1885 J.D.B. Stillman built his winery just south of Colton Avenue, now the site of Larsen Hall on the University of Redlands campus. The Stillman home, left, is the site of the Administration Building.

The Columbia sails in the pond at the Vaché's Brookside Winery, at the foot of Winery Grade (Fern Avenue), San Timoteo Canyon, c. 1905. Emile Vaché began this winery in 1884, and production began at Vaché Freres on October 10, 1885. The ranch was 178 acres.

The Haight Fruit Company, located in Redlands, was a marketing organization best known for citrus fruits. This rare advertisement was printed by H.S. Crocker & Co., a San Francisco lithography firm, in the late 1890s to advertise their California raisins. Crocker is one of several lithography companies to produce citrus labels. Rose Brand was later used to market citrus fruits by the Redlands Orange Growers Association.

In addition to grapes, dried fruit, consisting mostly of sulphured apricots, spawned many businesses. Pictured is Arthur Gregory's drying yard around 1890, with crews seen cutting fresh fruit and emptying trays of dried fruit.

Homer P.D. Kingsbury became known as the "marmalade king." Shown here is a view of his Kingsbury Fruit Factory, just after the turn of the century.

Founded in 1907, Joseph C. Kubias's olive oil company was constructed at the corner of Alta Street and Lugonia Avenue. "Bohemian Club Olive Oil," the name under which he marketed it, was sold throughout the southwestern United States.

Here is a young Washington navel orange grove in southwest Redlands, c. 1890. Parcels were often sold in 5-, 10-, and 20-acre sections. Navel orange groves were commonly owned by wealthy winter residents and out-of-state investors.

Imported from Brazil and sent to Southern California as a novelty, the seedless Washington navel orange took to the San Bernardino Valley climate and soil. This young tree bears "gold" for its owners. Soon navels from the "Citrus Belt" of Corona, Riverside, Redlands, Highland, San Bernardino, and Colton were being shipped all over the United States.

A grove worker picks ripe fruit during the harvest of navels in winter, 1912. Early in the history of citrus, Chinese and later Japanese immigrants were employed to harvest fruit. At the beginning of the 20th century, widespread recruitment of young men took place in the Midwest. By World War I, the political disruptions in Mexico led to the hiring of Mexican labor. Immigrants were used primarily because they were a cheap source of labor.

A young man inspects with a magnifying glass the quality of fruit just picked for Elephant Orchards in 1912. The field boxes shown in the picture have the Elephant Brand trademark imprinted on the box heads.

The children of the grove owner or visitors are carefully posed on a field box in this publicity photo taken during the navel orange harvest.

Charles Van Leuven sits atop his wagon hauling 212 empty field boxes on Brookside Avenue on May 16, 1912. The picking ladders on top are marked "Redlands Orange Growers Association."

The Redlands Mutual Orange Company, shown here around 1910 and not to be confused with Pure Gold, was one of several cooperatives formed by local growers. During the first two decades of the 20th century, the competition between them was fierce and often led to members not socializing with one another.

This classic packing house interior shows the transition in crews from men to women. Up to the present day, women make up nearly the entire staff of workers on the line. The importance of good line employees lies in their ability to judge the quality and size of the oranges, a technique also known as grading.

On December 17, 1923, the Gold Banner Association packing house on Central Avenue and Seventh Street burned to the ground in a fire that began in the sweat room (where fruit is stored before packing and, if necessary, can be treated to ripen artificially or bring out color) and caused an estimated $100,000 in damage. Manager Charles M. Brown vowed to rebuild the structure, and this time brick was used instead of wood.

Redlands Foothill Groves, a cooperative citrus association, was founded in 1924. This packing house was located at the northeast corner of Central Avenue and Sixth Street, next door to the "new" Gold Banner Association building. This view dates to around 1947. In 1948 the cooperative moved to a new facility on Ninth Street adjacent to the Santa Fe Railway tracks. In 2003, Redlands Foothill Groves became the last packing house left in Redlands still packing fruit.

By the Great Depression of the 1930s, women working on the line were largely Mexicans and Mexican Americans. This view, from the mid-1940s, shows Tom Peppers's packing house, where work is underway packing under the popular (and now collectible) Red Mule Brand label.

The freeze during the first days of January 1913 caused temperatures to plummet to as low as 23 degrees Fahrenheit. It denuded many of the orange trees, drove some growers into bankruptcy, and set back the Redlands economy until World War I. Orchard heaters, like those pictured in this 1949 snow scene, were not yet an industry standard.

Dissatisfied with the operations of the California Citrus Union, a cooperative experiment, a group of men representing leading citrus growers and packing houses led by Arthur Gregory Sr. met at the CCU office at 112 East State Street to hammer out the details of "a plan of complete and true cooperation that would benefit everyone from the grower through the packer and the seller." Mutual Orange Distributors (MOD), the product of this meeting, became one of the most influential organizations in the citrus industry, and Sunkist's largest competitor. Pure Gold initially was the designation MOD gave to top-quality fruit, and the designation became so synonymous with the company that for its golden anniversary MOD was officially renamed Pure Gold. In 1989 Pure Gold ceased operation.

Following the first citrus fair in Riverside in 1879, the popularity of displaying Southern California's "Gold Above Ground" as a marketing tool spread throughout the region. At the 1891 citrus fair in Los Angeles, Redlands's exhibit modeled the Bear Valley Dam (now Big Bear), then only six years old.

The most famous of Southern California's citrus fairs was the National Orange Show in San Bernardino, which began in tents at Fourth and D Streets in 1911. Citrus belt cities from Ontario to Riverside, and from Corona to East Highlands, exhibited their wares in elaborate displays. Redlands won first prize for its exhibit in 1965.

Five

REDLANDS, THE TOURIST MECCA

Railroads brought winter tourists to Redlands by the thousands. Major draws, promoted by the railroads and the local board of trade, included the stunning vistas of snow-capped peaks and moderate weather, oranges, and Cañon Crest Park.

The ill-fated Terracina Hotel opened for business in 1888 on the site now occupied by the Redlands Community Hospital. It burned under "suspicious circumstances" in 1895, ranking it among the greatest fires in the city's history.

The Atchison, Topeka, and Santa Fe Railway Company arrived in Redlands in 1888. This station, built in 1909–1910 by the Redlands Board of Trade (now the Redlands Chamber of Commerce) for the railroad, was designed by the San Francisco firm Bakewell and Brown, architects of San Francisco's post-1906 earthquake City Hall.

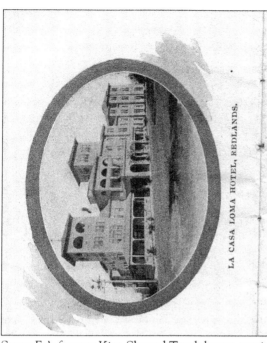

LA CASA LOMA HOTEL, REDLANDS.

The Loop, Redlands

This smaller eastward circle of the Kite-Shaped Track takes you through Redlands, noted for beautiful villas and navel oranges. Smiley Heights and Canyon Crest Park are located in its suburbs, and the view to be had from their commanding position, amid the bloom and fragrance of gardens and groves, is worthy an extended visit. From Redlands the loop circles to the north and west through groves of the finest navel oranges on the face of the globe. Here, too, is had a nearer view of the huge scarred surface of San Gorgonio and San Bernardino peaks, looming grandly, majestically to the heavens, rich with the magic waters that produce the fragrant bloom and fruit of the orchards below.

Santa Fe's famous Kite-Shaped Track began service to Redlands in 1892. The name comes from the kite-shaped horse race track. The smaller eastern circle of the line, which included the east San Bernardino Valley, was known as "the Loop."

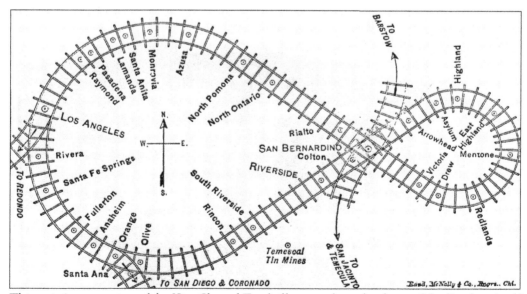

This artist's conception of the Kite-Shaped Track illustrates how the shape of the line lent itself to the name.

The mighty Southern Pacific laid its main line through San Timoteo Canyon in 1876, five years before Redlands was founded. Not to be outdone by Santa Fe, SP first bought the narrow-gauge motor line that ran into Redlands from San Bernardino, then laid standard-gauge track in 1891 and began regularly scheduled passenger service.

Southern Pacific built a new station along its main line through San Timoteo Canyon in 1924. The cost of the new station, including platforms, double-tracking, and other work, was more than $100,000. Located at the intersection of Fern Avenue and the tracks, it quietly opened on October 1, 1924. A major celebration event for the official opening took place 10 days later. Sadly, the station was open less than 30 years and was razed in the 1950s.

Fierce competition between Southern Pacific and Santa Fe was fueled by freight profits and, in Southern California, by burgeoning citrus production. Tourism in the late 1880s led to a ticket rate war with $1 fares for a trip from Chicago to Los Angeles. In order to compete with Santa Fe's famous Kite-Shaped Track for tourists in the Redlands-Riverside-San Bernardino area, Southern Pacific created the "Inside Track" tour.

LA CASA LOMA
REDLANDS, CAL.
JAS. S. AURAND.

Luncheon

SOUP
Vegetable Soup   Consomme en Tasse

RELISHES
Ripe Olives   Chow Chow   Yucaipa Radishes
Pearl Onions   Sour Gherkins

FISH
Baked Sea Bass, Allemande
Potatoes Brabant

ENTREES
Roast Winter Lamb, Plain or Mint Sauce
Baked Pork and Beans, Brown Bread
Fried Serf Fish, Tomato Sauce
Fig Fritters, Almond Sauce

VEGETABLES
Baked Potatoes   German Fried Potatoes
Stewed Corn   Rice   Creamed Spinach

String Bean Salad   Dressed Lettuce

COLD MEATS
Roast Beef   Premium Ham   Chipped Beef   Lamb
Corned Beef   Boneless Sardines   Salmi
Pickled Lambs Tongue

DESSERT
Orange Pudding
Apple Pie   Assorted Cake   Strawberry Sherbet
Apples   Bananas   Oranges   Fard Dates

American, Pineapple, Neufchatel and Edam Cheese
Water Crackers   Cupid Chips

Milk   Tea   Coffee   Cocoa

TUESDAY, MARCH 8, 1910.

La Casa Loma officially opened its doors on February 25, 1896, in time for the opening of the winter tourist season. Redlands was fast becoming a winter playground for East Coast and Midwest residents looking to avoid the harsh winters. The hotel changed proprietors several times over the years and, in December 1917, was renamed the Nichewaug, a name that did not stick. The Great Depression ended Redlands's time as a tourist destination.

The hotel is shown here as it appeared soon after completion, with the palm trees along Colton Avenue recently planted.

The Casa Loma was acquired by the University of Redlands, which used the structure as a women's residence hall and renamed it University Hall. In 1955 the university elected to develop the property.

The hotel was razed in 1955 to make way for Stater Bros. Supermarket and its parking lot.

Arthur Gregory Sr. built La Posada (The Hotel) at the northwest corner of State and Orange Streets. Construction began in 1930, and it officially opened September 12, 1931. The first-floor facade was "modernized" with brick in the early 1960s for the United States National Bank.

La Posada has been the subject of much discussion and lamentation. It was demolished in 1975 to make way for a parking lot for the Redlands Mall. An earlier "downtown revitalization" proposal incorporated the hotel and the Elks Club, also on West State Street. By the early 1970s, that plan was supplanted by one which leveled the structures in the area between Eureka and Orange Streets as well as Redlands Boulevard and Citrus Avenue—half of downtown.

Redlands, Cal.
Jan. 26, 1920

Dear Sara—

   I wish you were here to enjoy this beaty [sic] with me. We rode to Smiley Heights yesterday. It is a wonderful Park with so many palms and beautiful flowers. You would think we were in Fairyland. Eating lots of oranges. With love,

Carrie

The Redlands Street Railway Company was organized in 1889 and promptly started mule-drawn streetcar service. The line was electrified and re-routed in 1899. In 1903 it was merged with the San Bernardino Valley Traction Company. The Redlands Central Railway, which operated its line on Brookside and Citrus Avenues (left), was incorporated in 1907, and began operation the following year as a competitor to the SBVT. Both companies were acquired by Henry E. Huntington's interests and were merged into Pacific Electric Railway when Huntington sold to Southern Pacific in the "Great Merger" of 1911.

At 5:30 a.m. Christmas Day, 1924, the Pacific Electric morning newspaper train to Redlands took the curve from San Bernardino Avenue to Orange Street too fast, and the car jumped the track. Motorman Ellis blamed heavy smudging overnight for the accident, which took the life of passenger Ralph Goldsmith, a Redlands baker, whose leg was caught under a steel windowsill when the car tipped.

Pacific Electric Railway began operating the "Orange Empire Trolley Trip" on January 3, 1915. Cars left the PE building at Sixth and Main Streets in downtown Los Angeles at 9 a.m. and traveled first to Riverside for a tour of Sherman Institute (now Sherman Indian High School), lunch at Mission Inn, and then on to Redlands for a tour of the city, including a carriage ride over Smiley Heights. The trip was made daily until 1924, when it was scaled back to Wednesdays and Sundays. It was discontinued in August 1929.

PACIFIC ELECTRIC RAILWAY COMPANY

This transfer is receivable only at transfer point indicated and is good for one continuous passage of person to whom issued, within Local Fare Limits of the line to which issued, if presented within 15 minutes after the time punched. Void if mutilated or punched for more than one transfer point, date or time.

SAN BERNARDINO-REDLANDS-RIVERSIDE LOCAL TRANSFER — Examine your transfer before leaving car. (OVER)

Limit	Transfer Point TWO	Transfer Point ONE	Emergency	A. B. C.	P.E.S.P. Station	3rd & A Sts.	3rd & D Sts.	4th & D Sts.	Santa Fe Station	San Bernardino	Orange & Citrus	Redlands	14th & Main	7th & Main	Riverside	N S E W	A.M. / P.M.
1	31																
2	2930	2728	2526	2324	2122	1920	1718	1516	1314	1112	9 10	7 8	5 6	3 4	1 2	Day of Month	Form E.T.1
3																	
4																	
5																	

B COC77

RETURN

Complimentary

Good for One Automobile Trip

VALLEY OF THE FALLS

to

REDLANDS

By the 1910s, horse-drawn carriages and tallyhos gave way to vehicles powered by the mighty internal combustion engine. Scenic automobile and bus tours departed for the San Bernardino Mountains, to Lake Arrowhead, Big Bear, over the Rim of the World Drive, and to Forest Falls and Forest Home, in the Valley of the Falls.

Motor Transit Company was founded in 1917 and served points all over Southern California. In 1930 it was acquired by Pacific Electric Railway, owned by Southern Pacific, with the SP depot on Orange Street serving as the bus station. The Union Stage Depot, above, was at 105–107 East Citrus Avenue.

Six

REDLANDS LOVES AN EVENT

A parade marches down East State Street, turning north onto Orange Street. Redlands loves nothing better than the excuse to host and decorate for an event, this one *c.*1910.

President William McKinley arrived in Redlands on May 8, 1901. After his train ride into town, he and Mrs. McKinley boarded a special carriage that took them to the Casa Loma Hotel, where he was greeted by California governor Henry T. Gage, both of whom addressed the assembled crowd from the front balcony of the hotel.

Following his oration at the Casa Loma, President McKinley, accompanied by Governor Gage, toured Redlands in Albert C. Burrage's carriage pulled by four white stallions. Here the carriage has just passed under the arch at State Street, which was decorated with palm fronds and oranges. Some 10,000 people turned out for his "California Welcome," the first official stop in the state.

President McKinley's carriage passes in front of Smiley Library. Antoinette Humphries, librarian at the time, spent hours cleaning and polishing the library in case the President might make an "inspection." He did not.

The bust of President William McKinley in Smiley Park was officially dedicated on Memorial Day 1903, although it was unveiled on May 7 during the visit of President Theodore Roosevelt. Teddy Roosevelt ascended to the presidency following McKinley's assassination in September 1901. William Couper of New York sculpted the bust in bronze. Wording on the granite pedestal indicates its purpose: "As a Tribute to the man, and a record of the event [of his visit to Redlands], this memorial was erected by the citizens of Redlands."

A large crowd gathered at the Casa Loma Hotel to hear "rough rider" President Teddy Roosevelt address them from atop the port cochere, May 7, 1903. When referring to the Mojave Desert, the President pronounced it "Mo-jave." School teacher Nellie Westland Seuss corrected him and the President good naturedly accepted this testing of presidential etiquette.

Festooned with bunting, the Union Bank Building at State and Orange Streets is almost hidden. The crowd is beginning to gather in anticipation of the arrival of the presidential contingent. A large portrait of Roosevelt adorns the top of the building.

A Chinese family awaits a glimpse of President Roosevelt, the mother standing out of the sun in the shade of an electrical pole adorned with flowers. The Chinese community was largely centered between West State and Stuart Streets, bounded by First and Third (then Sylveria) Streets.

Albert Smiley, standing in front of his home in Cañon Crest Park, greets his friend, President Theodore Roosevelt. This photo became the standard press photo of Roosevelt's first stop in California. Harrison Gray Otis of the Los Angeles Times reportedly expressed shock and dismay that Redlands had out-scooped Los Angeles two presidential visits in a row with the presidents' first California stops at Redlands.

President William Howard Taft was the first president to tour Redlands by automobile, arriving October 12, 1909. Speaking from his car in front of the Casa Loma Hotel, he opened his talk by greeting the people of Riverside! This undoubtedly cost him votes in Redlands.

Journeying down west Citrus Avenue at Third Street, President Taft waved to Redlanders. His visit was cut short by the Secret Service because of groundless rumors that Willie Boy, a Native American wanted for a desert murder and being chased by three posses, might surprise the President and take a shot at him. Such speculation by the local press may have been an antidote to their boredom in covering the Taft visit.

The 60 guests at the Fishers' 1914 Turkish Costume Party were seated on cushions and ate from low tables set in the atrium, which was festooned with flags of many countries. After dinner, guests adjourned to the art gallery, with its ballroom and small stage, for entertainment and dancing.

Redlands's love for parades included, in the 1920s and 1930s, a children's flower parade. Shown here, walking through Smiley Park near the Redlands Bowl, are boys pulling a floral float with a girl sitting amongst the flowers.

The "Midsummer Night's Dream" street dance was in full swing on west State Street, around 1920. The street was closed off and illuminated, with a band playing lively music.

A parade marches south on Orange Street, crossing Redlands Boulevard, around 1948. An identifiable building is the 1892 Phinney Block, with its classic pointed pediment.

Richard M. Nixon visited Redlands while on the campaign trail in his controversial 1950 U.S. Senate race against Helen Gahagan Douglas. Nixon was familiar with Redlands, having debated against University of Redlands teams while a student at Whittier College. Perched atop the tailgate of his Ford, he orates to the crowd in front of the Triangle at Orange Street and Citrus Avenue.

Eleanor Roosevelt, America's First Lady, visits Redlands on her April 5, 1940 tour, with (left) Elam J. Anderson, president of the University of Redlands, and Harold C. Harris, an owner of the Harris Company department store. Mrs. Roosevelt spoke at a convocation at the university and visited numerous Redlands sites, charming everyone along the way.

81

An excited Charlie M. Brown, "senior fruit shipper and dynamic Democrat," enthusiastically bids bon voyage to Evelyn "Pinky" Kilgore Brier, whose small plane took off from west Central Avenue bound for Los Angeles in Redlands's first air mail flight, May 19, 1938.

Marjorie Fargo Smith entertains Redlands residents dressed in the costume of an earlier era with her portable organ during the celebration of Redlands's Golden Jubilee in 1938, marking the 50th anniversary of the incorporation of the city.

Members of Redlands American Legion Post 106 lead off the parade honoring the City of Redlands's Diamond Jubilee as it heads down Orange Street and turns east onto Citrus Avenue on a clear afternoon, November 9, 1963. The buildings on the left were razed for the Redlands Mall in the 1970s. The Academy of Music building, at right, survived.

A marching band entertains the Diamond Jubilee crowd on Orange Street. Unseen in the distance is the recently completed Interstate 10, a physical divider that, for some, created a psychological separation of the town.

Redlands Fourth of July Band conductor Curtiss Allen Sr. directs the band in "Put Me Off at Redlands," with vocal lead supplied by Mayor Carole Beswick. The occasion, which took place at Ed Hales Park, State and Fifth Streets, is the sit-down lunch for 1,000 people during the City of Redlands Centennial Celebration, November 22, 1988.

Cyclists rush north on Fourth Street, past the Lincoln Memorial Shrine in 1998. Begun in 1985, the annual Redlands Bicycle Classic, volunteer inspired and run, attracts teams from international competitions.

Seven

A CITY OF BEAUTIFUL HOMES

Frank Percey, in his "Beautiful Redlands Homes and Views," *Scenic America*, September, 1912, commented that Redlands is primarily a "city of beautiful homes." From its beginnings, the city's architectural styles, sizes, and shapes varied. This street scene features the Lee Wilmarth home in the center, with an unpaved Olive Avenue near the intersection of Nordina Street, right, and Sixth Street, left, around 1900.

The homes on Eureka Street in this photo taken May 5, 1913, across from A.K. Smiley Public Library, are typical of the cottages that lined the downtown streets.

By 1900 roses had become the favorite flower of Redlanders, as this *c.* 1910 scene of the block on Cajon Street between Home Place and Fern Avenue illustrates. Among the favorites were climber roses "Gold of Ophir," "Lady Banks," "Cecil Bruner," and "Cherokee."

Because the Lugonia area of Redlands, referred to from the 1950s forward as the "north side," had been settled in the 1870s, much of its property was already in agriculture and remained so. The wealthy winter residents from the east favored the south slopes of Redlands, while those permanent residents who held the jobs in business and agriculture lived in cottages like this newly built home at 519 East Stuart. Pictured is the Hite McMillin family around 1911.

William Lenox sits on the front porch while his wife stands in the garden of their home at 506 West Colton Avenue, later occupied by the Assistance League service building. Many people, whether of modest income or great wealth, took pride in and spent much time on their grounds, the theory being that yards were to be a shared visual delight.

HOMESEEKERS'

This was part of an advertising campaign in 1901, used by the Redlands Chamber of

Commerce in an attempt to bring settlers to the area.

When the Smiley Brothers began their grounds improvement contest in 1896—with cash prizes for owners of modest homes who adorned their grounds with plants—the J.T. Jordan home on Chestnut Avenue at Monterey Street took the prize.

From the tower of the Kingsbury School, a mule-drawn streetcar passes the Alexander residence on Cypress Avenue near Fourth Street. The presence of orange trees in this 1891 photo illustrates how many of the houses were set amidst groves, a common arrangement through the 1920s, when new subdivisions took over the area.

David and Sarah Morey built her dream home in 1890 using the $20,000 Mrs. Morey had made selling seedling navel orange trees to Matthew Gage of Riverside. Mrs. Morey died only a few years later, and Mr. Morey committed suicide, due to a painful illness, in San Diego. The property passed on to the Cheney family, and actress Carol Lombard, niece of Mrs. Cheney, spent many summers here as a girl.

The Fisk home was completed just in time for newlyweds John and Elizabeth Fisk to move in during December 1890. A once-typical grove home, it sits amidst five acres of Washington navel oranges. The Fisks substantially modified the house several times, adding on in 1900, 1911, and again in 1919.

Designed by T.R. Griffith, the 1895 home of Bernard H. Jacobs featured a tower and many porches. In 1908 the property was purchased by Andrew N. Dike, a partner in the firm that developed much of early-day Yucaipa.

Cornelia Hill built this house near Prospect Hill in 1897. In 1905 the property was sold to Mr. and Mrs. J. Alfred Kimberly, cofounder of the Kimberly-Clark Corporation. The estate was named Kimberly Crest, and was occupied by their daughter Mary Kimberly Shirk until her death in 1979, when the home passed to the Kimberly-Shirk Association, which maintains it as a house museum today.

The elegant mansion of Anthony G. and Laura Spoor Hubbard was originally built as the Terrace Villa Hotel, opening on December 26, 1886 and purchased by Hubbard in 1893. During the Depression of the 1890s, the mining millionaire created a beautiful home that was the scene of elegant parties. It became a school before being razed in 1961.

Henry Fisher, an immigrant from Prussia, came to Pennsylvania and made a fortune in the oil pipeline business. Arriving in Redlands, he invested in streetcar lines and was a founder of Southern California Edison. In 1897–1898, he and his socialite wife, Marion, built an elaborate Moorish mansion, complete with a separate art gallery. It was razed in the early 1940s.

The Davis home, known as "the Alders," was built in 1888, north of Brookside Avenue and east of Tennessee Street. The famous "new moon parties" given by hostess Jennie Davis induced the *Los Angeles Times* to feature the grounds and social events. Scheduled for demolition for a strip mall in 1978, the house was moved to Rialto for a business and substantially altered.

In 1896, with a fortune made from manufacturing candy, Alonzo and Irene Hornby built a mansion on Highland Avenue at Crown Street. The Hornby family participated in many Redlands philanthropies, including funds for a building at the University of Redlands. It was destroyed by fire on April 21, 1953, just 11 days after the Albert K. Smiley home in Smiley Heights burned to the ground.

Charles Kendall Adams served as president of Cornell University and the University of Wisconsin and was a nationally known historian. When his health failed, he and his wife came to Redlands and built this Italianate home, "Kendall Place," on Palm Avenue, but they lived there less than six months before he passed away.

Gertrude Hicks had patents for metal tips for shoelaces, a carry-out delicatessen carton, and one version of the snap-on clothespin. Oliver H. Hicks invented a process for corrugated paper. Their home, Allview, was built in 1906 and featured hidden wall panels for Mrs. Hicks's jade collection.

The Phelps Stokes mansion was designed in Mediterranean style by architect Isaac Newton Phelps Stokes for his aunts Olivia and Caroline Phelps Stokes. The Phelps Stokes were heirs to the Phelps Dodge Corporation and the Stokes publishing empire, and were philanthropists of great note nationally. In Redlands, Olivia Phelps Stokes gave the land for Caroline Park in honor of her sister, as well as the gates at Hillside Memorial Park, which were designed by Isaac Newton Phelps Stokes and constructed by Samuel Yellin.

The Albert Cameron Burrage estate was completed in time for his family's winter arrival in 1901. Burrage made a fortune in copper and with Standard Oil, and constructed this home for a winter "party house," complete with a polo field. Charles Brigham, a Boston architect, designed the Mission Revival structure without ever coming to California and seeing a mission.

George W. Bowers made a fortune in the mines of Arizona as a partner of Anthony G. Hubbard, and built this mansion on West Crescent Avenue. Note not only the classical columns, but also the ornately carved furniture, popular in the 1880s. Sadly, this home has suffered great damage as the result of fire.

William F. Holt was the developer of the Imperial Valley and founder of El Centro and Holtville, which was to be the "Redlands of the Imperial Valley." His home is one of the best examples of Moorish style architecture in Southern California. Constructed in 1904, it boasts a single lane Brunswick bowling alley in the basement.

Built for New York attorney Kirke H. Field and his wife, Myra Howard, daughter of Mark Howard, the founder of the Hartford Fire Insurance Company. This English Tudor-style cottage was constructed in 1908 and named "Mira Flores." The Fields were generous patrons of Redlands education and social life.

Pasadena architects and builders the Greene brothers, among others, helped popularize the California Craftsman Bungalow, a style that became popular in Redlands. Built in 1911 for C.H. Williams and designed by Robert B. Ogden, this home on Cypress Avenue at Alvarado Street is typical of Redlands's love affair with Craftsman homes.

Bungalow Section Eureka Street, Redlands, California.

S-292

During the 1910s and 1920s, the Craftsman bungalow was the rage, with entire neighborhoods constructed by builders like Garrett Huizing, a native of Holland. These homes are on Eureka Street, north of Cypress Avenue.

This chamber of commerce advertisement from a 1914 publication celebrating the new building of the First National Bank of Redlands describes the wonders of "Redlands for Residence."

By the 1950s the popular ranch-style home in tracts and custom lots were consuming orange groves by the dozens.

The tract house became a staple of Redlands housing stock from the 1950s on. The population of the city grew from 19,000 in 1949 to 30,000 by 1960 and 60,000 in 1990. It continues to grow as more groves are turned into housing developments.

Eight

FROM KINDERGARTEN
TO COLLEGE

This is Mary Eccles's first-grade class in 1929–1930. From its beginnings, Redlands had a diverse population, encompassing people of many backgrounds and ethnicities.

Construction of a new Lugonia School started in 1908, using bricks from the Taylor brickyard. Working on the crew is Willie Boy (second from left), who would be accused the following year of murdering a man and, according to sensationalized press accounts, his girlfriend. He was chased through the desert by three posses in "the last great western manhunt."

This shows Lugonia School four years after it was completed. The school burned just after Christmas 1963.

This is an early view of Maria Witmer's fourth- and fifth-grade class at Lincoln School, around 1905. Witmer served as principal of the school in addition to teaching. Lincoln School stood on Colton Avenue, between Texas and Lawton Streets.

Constructed in 1901, Barton School took its name from pioneer Ben Barton and was located north of the Barton House on Nevada Street.

McKinley School, at the southeast corner of Olive Avenue and Center Street, was built in 1903 and razed in 1937.

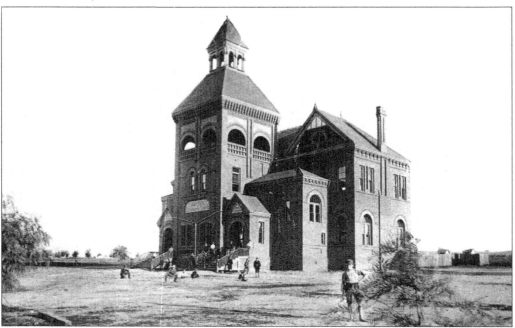

The first Kingsbury School was completed at the southwest corner of Cypress Avenue and Cajon Street in 1888.

The second Kingsbury School cornerstone was laid June 1, 1925, and construction was completed the following December at a cost of $135,000. There were 13 classrooms with a total pupil capacity of 480, a significant expansion from the previous school building.

The second Kingsbury School was demolished in May 1969. California's Field Act required that public schools built before the Act had to be retrofit to new earthquake standards or phased out of use.

The students of Mission School pose for a class photo on the front steps in 1923.

Lincoln School was designed in the popular Mission Revival style, an architectural movement inspired by Helen Hunt Jackson's novel *Ramona: A Story*, published in 1884. A new school was built there in 1941 as a WPA project.

Lowell Grammar School, also known as the State Street School, was built in the early 1900s on Church Street at East Citrus Avenue. It later would be the site of Redlands Junior High School.

Redlands Junior High School was built between east State Street and Citrus Avenue at Church Street. Following the opening of E.M. Cope Junior High School in 1958, it became part of the Redlands High School campus and was razed in the late 1960s for new campus buildings.

Students play football on the field next to the original Redlands Union High School building, built in 1893 and enlarged in 1896.

The foundation and brick walls of the new high school building take shape in 1904. The original building is the left third of the new structure, modified into the new design.

This shows the high school's new building as it appeared in 1912. A major building campaign began in the mid-1950s, resulting in the razing of this structure and several other older buildings.

Here is the Manual Arts building on the Redlands High School campus in March 1912. It stood along the Fern Avenue section of the campus, before the street was closed for more campus space in 1965.

The University of Redlands was founded in 1907 as a Northern Baptist university. Following the disastrous 1906 San Francisco earthquake, the Baptists began looking for a location away from the Bay Area. When they decided on Redlands, they had no idea of its proximity to the San Andreas Fault. The Greek Revival Administration Building was completed in 1909, and the President's Mansion, to the east, in 1910. Sitting atop the mower in Sylvan Park is Tom Lloyd.

The University of Redlands choir, conducted by Professor William Olds, poses in front of the mighty "Sermon on the Mount" or "Christ Window," created by the famous Judson Studios of Los Angeles, in the Memorial Chapel.

The Memorial Chapel, listed in the National Register of Historic Places, was designed by architect and alumnus Herbert Powell and built in 1927. The Georgian tower is framed in the background by Mt. Harrison and the San Bernardino mountain range with a dusting of winter snow.

Navy V-12 units drill on the Quad in front of the Chapel. In 1943–1944, 631 men were part of the program, which brought the university's enrollment to 1,214, the largest enrollment up to that point. In addition to the V-12's 29-hours-per-week class requirement were drills before breakfast and marching drills in the afternoon.

The annual University of Redlands Pajamarino was begun October 6, 1911. Parading from campus down Colton Avenue and south on Orange Street, the group would end up at the Redlands Bowl or inside the Fox Theater for a brief rally. Urbanization caused the event to be cancelled in the 1970s.

The University of Redlands Air Show was held on October 26, 1911. A Bleriot monoplane is on the field, approximately where Fairmont and Anderson Halls stand on the University Quad. The Administration Building can be seen in the distance.

Nine

A CITY OF CULTURE AND PHILANTHROPY

Greeting Andrew Carnegie (left), then the richest man in the world, his friend Albert K. Smiley welcomes him to Cañon Crest Park on March 19, 1910. Smiley's niece Ruth remembered the visit and Carnegie's interest in the beautiful views. Carnegie's daughter Margaret wrote in her journal about the "delightful visit with dear old Mr. Smiley."

SMILEY MEMORIAL EDITION   PRICE TEN CENTS

The Citrograph.

VOL. XXXII.—No. 7.   REDLANDS, CAL., SATURDAY, FEBRUARY 28, 1903.   WHOLE No. 816.

ALFRED H. SMILEY   ALBERT K. SMILEY

COMPLIMENTS OF
JOHN P. FISK,
Real Estate Agent.
REDLANDS, · CAL.

This portrait of identical twin brothers Alfred H. Smiley (seated) and Albert K. Smiley became the standard image utilized in magazines and in the press when writing about the two educators, resort owners, and philanthropists. Alfred Smiley's death in February 1903 caused much sadness in Redlands and was the occasion of this special Memorial Edition of *The Citrograph*.

This is the most famous and widely used publicity photograph of Smiley Heights, Redlands, and Mount San Bernardino in the distance. Taken around 1900 from A.K. Smiley's bedroom window, this view lured thousand of tourists to visit Southern California and especially to Redlands.

A woman inspects the Shasta daisies by Mirror Lake in Cañon Crest Park. The distinctive "summer houses" were replicas of the ones at the Smiley brothers' resorts at Lake Mohonk and Lake Minnewaska, New York. Redlands locals called the buildings "spooners" after the practice known as "spooning" in which young folks sat, gazed into each other's eyes, and kissed.

This photograph, taken around 1910, shows two children walking down a path along San Timoteo Canyon in Cañon Crest Park. The dense forest of deodar cedars, native to the Himalayas, was a favorite among visitors to the park. In his volume on Southern California from his widely read world travel series, John L. Stoddard referred to the park as the "converted mountain, an incomparable hill, the whole of which has been, as if by magic, metamorphosed into an estate, where visitors are allowed to find instruction and delight upon its lofty terraces of forest and flowers."

A view from Crest Road looking west to A.K. Smiley's house in Cañon Crest Park. The house, completed in 1891 and designed by Redlands architect Corydon B. Bishop, is framed by the San Timoteo Canyon "Badlands" in the background. The house burned in 1953.

Albert K. Smiley stands in Cañon Crest Park by a tallyho filled with friends heading to Riverside in 1903 for the dedication of the new Sherman Institute. Smiley, a member of the U.S. Board of Indian Commissioners, proved influential in having the school named for James Schoolcraft Sherman, New York congressman and later Taft's vice president.

This April 1898 view of the about-to-be-dedicated A.K. Smiley Public Library features its Moorish-inspired architecture and central observation tower. Albert K. Smiley borrowed $60,000 to purchase the park and build the library, which he gifted to the City of Redlands. On April 28, 1898, the *Redlands Daily Facts* wrote that the library's tower was designed for electric lighting, which would signify the library's mission: "to give the light of knowledge freely to all who make use of its free privileges."

Albert Smiley provided funds to expand the reference wing in 1906. The east wall was dismantled, stained glass and all, and reassembled in its new location. The top floor and roof of the tower were removed in 1936 due to seismic concerns brought about by the disastrous 1933 Long Beach earthquake.

Because architect Elmer Grey felt the library's red color overpowered his Lincoln Memorial Shrine, just south of the library, he urged prominent philanthropist Robert Watchorn in 1939 to paint the library white.

Completed in early 2003, the library's exterior restoration project returned the library to its original look. The tower had been rebuilt in 1999 through a private fundraising campaign, and the white paint, which caused problems from years of trapped moisture and a leaky roof, was removed and redone. The red slurry restores the building's Moorish look.

The name "Prosellis" was coined by the donors of the building, Clarence and Florence White. It comes from the Latin pro, meaning "before," and sellis, meaning "seats," as the classical structure stands "before the seats." Donated in 1930 and designed by local architect Herbert Powell, the Redlands Bowl Prosellis hosts more than 100,000 people per season during the Redlands Community Music Association's summer musical series.

Feb, 5 & 6 30 4.

SEASON 1903-1904

THE SPINET

CHILDREN'S OPERETTA

"The Queen's Surprise"

In Charge of
Mrs. Spoor and Mrs. Fisher

❧

Y. M. C. A. Auditorium
February 5 and 6, 1904, 3:30 p. m.

The Spinet was formed on October 15, 1894, at the home of Margaret Howard White. It is the oldest federated musical organization in California. The Redlands Orchestra had formed in May 1888, and in 1905 the Spinet began a concert series. When Edward C. Tritt founded the Redlands Symphony Orchestra in 1950, it was rooted in a long tradition. The symphony, a true town and gown project, has prospered because of Redlands's musical tradition.

The Lincoln Memorial Shrine was given as a gift to the City of Redlands in 1932 by Robert Watchorn (left). As a young boy, Watchorn worked in the coal mines of central England and immigrated to the United States at 22 in search of a better life. He worked in coal mines in Pennsylvania, became the secretary of the United Mine Workers, and later was appointed to the U.S. Immigration Service, rising to commissioner of immigration at Ellis Island. After the election of Taft, he found himself in need of employment and became secretary of the Union Oil Company, later founding the Watchorn Oil and Gas Company.

The Lincoln Memorial Shrine was designed by prominent Southern California architect Elmer Grey and was constructed of Indiana limestone, with interior murals by noted illustrator Dean Cornwell. This 1937 scene of the memorial shows the recently completed fountain wings. Designed and sculpted by Merrill Gage, sculptor professor at the University of Southern California, the fountains feature colored night lighting.

Formed in 1896, the Redlands Country Club is the second oldest country club in Southern California and the oldest still on its original site. It expanded to 18 holes in 1926 with the counsel of noted course designer Alister MacKenzie.

The University Club was founded in 1902 to promote cordiality among its members and to further university interests. Albert Burrage, a charter member of the club, donated the lots on which the University Club was built in 1904 at Fern Avenue and Cajon Street.

Jennie Davis Park on Redlands Boulevard at New York Street is a memorial to Jennie Davis, Redlands pioneer and advocate for civic beautification. In 1937 the women of the Contemporary Club advocated a park on the site of the city dump, known as the "Glory Hole," at the west entrance to Redlands. "If only those damned women would have waited a few years, we could have filled it," lamented city engineer George Hinckley after the park was dedicated in 1945.

The Redlands Horticultural and Improvement Society began annual flower shows in 1913. They were initially held in the Contemporary Club at Fourth and Vine Streets, as illustrated by this photo from one of the earliest shows.

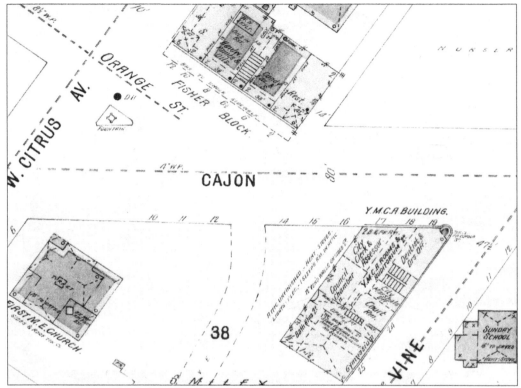

Numerous, too, are lesser-known individuals who helped to create park space for all to enjoy. Forest Waycott, S.L. Graw, and W.F. Allison granted the Triangle to the city in 1887. The Triangle was created by the intersection of Orange Street and Citrus Avenue, perpendicular to each other, and then Cajon Street, which intersected them at an angle. It was granted to Edward Judson in trust for Redlands "to be used for public purposes, as a public fountain and watering place." Cajon and Orange Streets were later re-engineered, and Cajon Street now curves to meet the intersection of Orange Street and Citrus Avenue. The Triangle, however, remains.

This shows the Triangle as it appeared in the early 1920s. "Meet me at the Triangle" was a common phrase, as its central location made it the perfect meeting spot. Later, the city allowed GTE to expand its building over the section of Cajon Street adjacent to the Triangle.

Here is Prospect Park as it looked on February 13, 1905. The England family created this Japanese-style fish pond on the crest of Prospect Hill. In the distance are the homes of Summit Avenue, with the Eldridge M. Lyon estate on the left and the Benton O. Johnson home on the right.

The subdivision and development of Cañon Crest Park beginning in 1962 motivated town residents to prevent the development of Prospect Park into a mobile home park. Through several campaigns and the leadership of many prominent Redlanders, including Mary Kimberly Shirk, Helen G. Fisk, and Avice Meeker Sewall, hundreds of citizens donated time and money to preserve it for the future. Leon and Margie Armantrout drive the Prospect Park entry in the 1963 Redlands Diamond Jubilee Parade.

Designed by Arthur Benton, one of the architects for the Mission Inn hotel in Riverside, the Contemporary Club served as the headquarters for the socially and culturally minded membership. Constructed in 1904, the building was razed in 1971 for the Vine Street widening project, which was never completed by the city. This photograph was taken April 19, 1913.

Founded by Kirke H. Field (seated in the front row, fourth from left) and the Reverend J.D. Easter in 1895, the Fortnightly Club is a literary club whose members read papers to each other on a wide variety of topics. It is one of the oldest literary societies in the United States. Here the membership appears at A.K. Smiley Public Library, April 1936.

The Kimberly Juniors pose with Helen Cheney Kimberly, founder of the KJs, at the Contemporary Club in 1922. The organization, formed in 1916, served as an adjunct of the Contemporary Club to give training for future community leadership.

Dedicated on Patron Saints's Day, March 17, 1991, the bronze statue of Alfred and Albert Smiley in Smiley Park was in large part made possible by funds from the Moore Historical Foundation. Shown here, from left to right, are William G. Moore, foundation founder and president; Frank E. Moore, foundation board member; and Linda Pew, the sculptor.

ACKNOWLEDGMENTS

These projects are never done alone. The board of trustees of A.K. Smiley Public Library provided encouragement for us to undertake this project. Colleagues helped with suggestions and criticism or wisely kept out of our way: Janice Jones, Brennan Gosney, Jana Halvorson, Don McCue, Allison Peyton, and Richard Hanks. Zitan Chen graciously translated the sign in the image of the First National Bank from Chinese to English.

It is only through the work of Redlands photographers that a project like this could be undertaken. Every image in this book was taken from the holdings of the photo and ephemera archives at A.K. Smiley Public Library. Thankfully, thousands of images have been saved over time and made their way to library holdings to be preserved for generations to come, helping to give enlightenment, interest, and a sense of place to the community. Photographers such as Elias Everett, C.N. Jackson, R.J. Phillipi, Barnett, Kline, and most certainly dozens of others whose photographs are unidentified, have accomplished something they may not have directly intended: providing a means for the combined history of a community over the course of 125 years to be documented, preserved, and shared.